The Origin of the Mound Builders

A Thesis

Alfred O. Coffin, M.A.

Originally Published in 1889

Table of Contents

The Mound-builders of the Mississippi Valley

The Mound-builders in Mexico

The Mound-builders in Central America

The Lost Atlantis

Deductions

The First Men of America

Conclusion

Alfred O. Coffin

I
The Mound-builders of the Mississippi Valley

"To ask or search, I blame thee not; for heaven is as the book of God before thee set, wherein to read his wondrous works."

Let any traveler start from Wisconsin and traverse the Mississippi Valley to the Gulf of Mexico, and cross the country from the Alleghenies to the Western Plateau, and throughout his course he will find thousands of mounds of earth with a conical or pyramidal apex, and containing within their interior relics of human remains and inventions.

When a traveler asks the origin and reasons of these mounds, he is almost invariably met with the enigmatical answer, "Indian mounds." They were not made by the Indians whom Columbus found on this continent; in fact, their origin was unknown to the Red Man, since they found them here, and they looked as recent to the first European adventurers, with the remains of ancient forests on their summits, as they do to us now.

When a boy, I have stood and wondered at the stupendous magnificence of the Mound-builders' rude art, in crowning a beautiful hill with a throne for their Chieftain, or perhaps a temple to their god of nature, or possibly a sacrificial altar, on which to shed human blood to appease an irate divinity, or to dedicate the triumphal march of a conquering hero. Since a man, I have wandered among the thousands of mounds, from the Great Lakes to the Mexican Gulf, and have pondered among the unclassified tumuli on the plains of Texas that stretch away toward the Rio Grande, and have wondered if these are the watch-towers of a gigantic antediluvian prairie-dog contemporaneous with the Deinosaurs, or if they are the mute landmarks of a mysterious people who trafficked here while Cheops was building on the Nile. While modern science is endeavoring to classify the ethnic relations of the Mound-builders, it is also aware that that hypothesis alone will have credence, that accords best with the cumulative evidence of those most infallible guides, comparative craniology and philology.

The science of craniology recognizes three, and sometimes four, kinds of skulls, determined by the ratio of length to the breadth; that is, the length of any skull being represented by 100, the "cephalic index" is the proportion of this 100 covered by the breadth. Skulls with a cephalic index between 74 and 78 are said to be mesocephalic, because this is the average of mankind. If the index is above 78, they are said to be brachycephalic; if below 74, they are dolichocephalic, or long-headed. The dolichocephalic, according to Prof. Retzius, are found in the eastern part of this continent, from Labrador through the Antilles to Paraguay. The brachycephali, or short heads, are found in the West, from Behring's Strait, through Oregon and California, Mexico, Central America and Chili, to Terra del Fuego. It must be remembered that the terms "brachycephalic" and "dolichocephalic" are not absolute, but only relative as to length and breadth, for a dolichocephalic cranium may be actually shorter than a brachycephalic one.

The Caribs, who inhabit the shores of the Caribbean Sea, are a nautical people, who conquered the Antilles, as is attested by their war implements being found there, and entered North America by the southeast, and spread north to Canada, giving rise to the red Indian, whose dolichocephalic skulls and roving habits agree precisely with the Caribs of Venezuela. The brachycephalic type is supposed to have entered America by Behring's Strait, giving rise to the Aleutians and Esquimaux, and passing through Washington Territory and California has characterized the Hualpa Indians of the latter, and the semi-civilized cliff-dwellers of Colorado and Pueblo Indians of New Mexico. The high degree of civilization which Cortez found in Mexico, the unnumbered temples of the Montezumas, the splendor of Toltec civilization, the paved roads of Peru, and the gilded palaces of the sun-worshipers of Lake Titicaca, all show that the brachycephalic civilization of the Pacific Slope was as distinct from the culture of the hunting tribes of the Atlantic, as though separated by an ocean. In the Chicago Academy of Science are a number of Mound-builders' skulls, taken from mounds in Ohio, Indiana, Kentucky and Illinois. There are no other skulls of any other race in this country like them—with scarcely any forehead whatever, but with a sudden slope from the superciliary ridges backward. These skulls are neither dolichocephalic nor brachycephalic; therefore we can neither look to the ancestry of the Red Men, nor to the Asiatic type, for the progenitors of the Mound-builders, who may justly be considered the autochthones of America.

Before attempting to account for the presence of the Mound-builders in the Mississippi Valley, we will describe a few of their mounds, the only history they have left us.

These mounds are divided into three classes, according to their use. The most northern remains of the Mound-builders yet discovered are on the southern shore of Lake Superior, and in the valley of the Wisconsin River. All of these mounds are representations of animals on a gigantic scale—hence we will call them effigy mounds—and seem to represent their religious rites. No other mounds are found here, which was not a place of residence, and this character of mound is not found elsewhere except the great Serpent Mound in Adams County, Ohio. Around Chicago the mounds are not more than twelve feet high, but in Iowa they were so plentiful that the French named the river in that State "Des Moines," which means "the mounds." Where St. Louis stands was once so thickly studded with mounds, that the city has been called "The Mound City." In the State of Mississippi the largest river was so thickly strewn with these prehistoric ruins that the Choctaws called it "Yazoo-okhinnah"—"The River of Ancient Ruins." In Illinois the mounds are oblong, square, ellipsoidal and conical. Cahokia, the largest mound in the United States, stood here. It formed a parallelogram with sides respectively seven hundred and five hundred feet long and ninety feet high, and covered fifteen acres—larger than the largest pyramid in Egypt. On the top of this mound was probably a temple, for many bones and funeral vases were taken from the interior; so we call this a temple mound. The banks of the Ohio, Scioto, Wabash and Muskingum are so thickly covered with mounds and tumuli, that Squier and Davis estimate that Ohio alone contains ten thousand, and plainly indicate that this was the capital of the Mound-builders' empire. A number of these are conical mounds, and the bones and charcoal indicate that they were sacrificial mounds. Near Newark, Ohio, occur the most stupendous of the Mound-builders' works, covering two square miles, and containing walls, pyramids, circles and turrets, which in our day, with machinery and horse-power, would require many thousand men many months to perform.

One of the wonders of the world is the great Serpent Mound in Adams County, Ohio, which stamps the religious character of the vanished race. The total length of the serpent is fourteen hundred and fifteen feet, and the distance between the jaws one hundred feet. It lies on the crest of a hill, and its folds correspond with the windings of the hill. Is this serpent an emblem of the one that plays such a part in the mythology of the old world? "This symbol prevails in Egypt, Greece, Assyria, and among the superstitions of the Celts, Hindoos and Chinese. Wherever native religions have had their scope, this symbol is sure to appear."

On the Ohio River, twelve miles from Wheeling, in West Virginia, stands the Grave Creek Mound, seventy feet high and a thousand feet in circumference. This was a signal mound, from the summit of which signal fires could be seen far down the valley, and others transmitted the message in like manner, till it reached Cahokia on the Mississippi.

The growth of civilization has always been along the courses of great rivers—the Nile, Euphrates, Ganges, Hoangho, Danube, the Mississippi and Ohio. The Mound-builders were an agricultural people, for maize has been found in the mounds, and nowhere do we find the mounds where maize will not grow. Where the population of the United States is growing densest every year, there, too, the Mound-builders reached their acme, showing that what we consider natural advantages so did they. Ohio, the second State in the Union, was likewise their capital, with its ten thousand mounds to-day marking the spot where flourished their vanished cities.

They were an agricultural people, because no other occupation could have supported so vast a concourse of people. Their government was despotic; for when we consider that they had no metallic tools or beasts of burden, but that these mounds were raised by earth scraped from the surface and carried up in baskets, we are bound to conclude that these mounds are the work of slaves; for, studying the history of Egypt, we know that no wealth or power on earth could have erected these pyramids by freemen working in competition for freemen's wages.

Two thousand men were employed three years in carrying a stone from Elephantis to Sais, and the building of one pyramid required the labor of three hundred and sixty thousand men for twenty years.

They understood political economy and the division of labor; else so many men could not have been fed, while their labor was withdrawn from production and locked up in this yearly labor, unless there was a powerful reserve force like Joseph to store the granaries in time of plenty.

They were a commercial people; for in these mounds we find copper from Lake Superior, shells from the Mexican Gulf, mica from the Alleghenies, iron pyrites from Missouri and obsidian from Mexico.

They were an inventive people; for we find specimens of cloth, woven from a vegetable fibre, in several different patterns; and they were not warlike, for most of the instruments taken from the mounds are of agricultural pattern. They were not of the same stock as the red Indian, because the Indian, even in the nineteenth century, is still in the Stone Age, roving in feral tribes, and starving to death annually rather than taint his inherited dignity by manual labor. The Indian's implements are of flint, and always on the surface of the ground. The Mound-builder's implements are of argillite, and found beneath the surface and gravel. The Indian's habitation is never durable enough to be traced by his succeeding progeny, while the Mound-builder has left his mark which ten thousand years will but intensify.

The Mound-builders can not be identified with the Pueblo Indians, because the pottery of the Puebloes is corrugated and indented, and never has the semblance of any animal form whatever; while that of the Mound-builders is striated, and eminently characterized by animal forms and statuettes of the human form divine. They can not be classed with the Esquimaux, because the Esquimaux are a strictly Orarian people, and we have no evidence of their ever having been aught else.

"The brain is the seat of mental activity, and we place the seat of the intellectual faculties in the anterior lobe; of the propensities which link us to the brute, in the middle lobe; and of those which appertain to the social affections, in the posterior lobe. The predominance of any one of these divisions in a people would stamp them as either eminently intellectual, eminently cruel, or eminently social." From an examination of the few authentic skulls of the Mound-builders, we are confident that these people were neither eminent for great virtues nor great vices, but were a mild, inoffensive race, who would fall an easy prey to a crafty and cruel foe. The Mound-builders entered the Mississippi Valley by way of Mexico, being drawn thither by the superior attraction of the soil and climate of our river terraces and bottoms, and they remained here until crowded out by the savage hunting tribes of red Indians, when they retraced their steps to Mexico and developed that higher intellectual and architectural skill which we will now consider.

And now, having hastily glanced at a very few of the tens of thousands of mounds familiar to every inhabitant of the Mississippi Valley, we will follow the trail of the Mound-builders as evinced by their works, through Phillips County, Arkansas, four miles from Helena, thence to Red River, where they disappear.

Taking up the trail again at the Hollywood plantation, near Saint Joseph, Louisiana, in Tensas Parish, we find ten mounds in a circle facing the temple. A few miles southward, facing Natchez, in Catahoula Parish, is another group. Crossing Louisiana, we enter Texas, and from the Trinity to the Colorado River there are millions of mounds, all of a conical form, that have baffled ethnologists for the last fifty years. They are from one to five feet in height, and from thirty to one hundred and forty feet in diameter. All scientists who have examined them have pronounced them the "inexplicable mounds." During the summer of '87 and '88 I have traveled for days among the same mysterious mounds in Texas, stretching in an unbroken line toward the Rio Grande, and have pronounced them "landmarks" that indicated the line of departure of the Mound-builders, in their migration across the treeless prairies.

This conclusion brings us to consider the Mound-builders after the migration, in their new home.

Alfred O. Coffin

II
The Mound-builders in Mexico

"Nations melt From Power's high pinnacle, when they have felt the sunlight for a while, and downwards go."

We know that the Mound-builders had a knowledge of Mexico before their southwestern migration, because obsidian was found in their mounds, and this mineral is found only in Mexico.

No links are so conclusive in connecting the Mound-builders of the Mississippi Valley with those of Mexico, as the truncated, pyramidal mounds. True to the historical traditions that all great centers of civilization have been along the great river basins, we would naturally turn to the water-courses of Mexico to resume the trend of our narrative, and we are not disappointed.

On the Panuca River, near the Gulf of Tampico, Mr. Norman found twenty-five mounds, some of them covering two acres, and built of earth as those in the Mississippi Valley, though some were faced with stones. According to the Smithsonian Report of 1873, across the river from Vera Cruz occurs a locality of mounds covering three square leagues. The pyramids of Papantla and Tuscapan are of solid masonry with steps on the outside. The pyramid of Cholula is truncated, its base being one thousand four hundred and twenty-three feet long, covering forty-four acres. Its perpendicular height is one hundred and seventy-two feet, and its truncated summit contains more than one acre; this was the Mecca of the valley of Anahuac. The hanging gardens of Tezcuco had a summit reached by five hundred and twenty steps and crowned by a fountain. Nezahualeoyotl built a pyramidal temple nine stories high, dedicated to "The Unknown God, the Cause of Causes." In the ruins of Mitla, Oaxaca, Guingola, and numerous others, we have numerous ruins of different construction; but to say that they are the works of different races of people is saying too much. All the inhabitants of Nahuac were kindred tribes, and spoke the Nahuatl language, though entering the valley at different times in different clans. Winchell states that the Mongoloids entered North America by Behring's Strait and spread east and southward; that the beginning of this wave is lost in obscurity, but in due succession the Nahuas moved forward. The Toltecs followed and crowded the Nahuas through the Isthmus of Tehuantepec into Yucatan and Central America. The Astecs followed the Toltecs in occupancy. While the Astecs crowded on the Toltecs, these pushed farther the Nahuas, and the Nahuas pressed on the rear of their unknown and mysterious predecessors, and so forth to the borders of Chili. Also another branch of Mongoloids entered South America by the Polynesian route, crossed the Andes, ascended the Atlantic Slope to the Caribbean Sea, crossed to the Antilles and entered North America by the Tortugas and Florida, ascended the Atlantic Slope and began war on the peaceful inhabitants of the Pacific Slope, when the white man arrived and interrupted this symmetrical rotation and sequence of invasion. I beg leave differ with regard to a part of this plan, on grounds adduced further on.

The Toltec clan was among the first to enter the Valley of Mexico or Nahua, followed by the Chichimecs, who were succeeded by the seven clans or tribes who dwelt in the valley at the same time, and who probably are connected with "the seven mysterious cities of Cibola" in New Mexico.

These tribes were the Xochimilcos, Cholcos, Tepanecos, Acolhuas, Tezcucans, Tlascaltecas and Astecs. For political strength the Astecs, Tezcucans and Tlascans formed a triumvirate, and each had their capital city, viz.: Tezcuco, Tlasca, and Tenochtitlan. The Astec clan in its peregrinations had kept the name Astec, in honor of their ancient home, Aztlan or Atlantis, but their priest, Aacatl, decreed that they should be called Mexicatls, in honor of their war god, Mexitli, because he had enabled them to conquer their brethren.

In the midst of the beautiful Lake Tezcuco, on an island, they built their national capital, Tenochtitlan, which the Spaniards called "the most beautiful spot on earth." Cortez destroyed this beautiful city and built the modern city of Mexico on its ruins. It was here that the ill-starred "Moteuczoma"—whom the Spaniards have misspelled Montezuma—poured the wealth of his kingdom into the coffers of Cortez, and in return suffered the most humiliating degradation and death recorded on the pages of history.

Tenochtitlan was a great city. Two thousand temples, one hundred palaces and a thousand sumptuous dwellings have melted before the desecrating Spaniards as a mirage before a thirsty traveler.

The priests, in their too zealous zeal to uproot polytheism, wreaked their holy vengeance upon temples and idols; and history can produce no parallel to the vandalism that would sack the temples of all the written documents and ideographic paintings and make a bonfire of them on the public plaza, on the plea that they were from the devil!

The zenith of New World civilization became a setting sun before a savage Christianity. The path of the Christian became a sirocco, the garden spot of the world became a holocaust.

Tenochtitlan, the city of palaces, the capital of the Valley of Anahuac, was razed to the ground, and the testimony of a thousand years of civilization was as completely lost to the modern world as the buried island of Atlantis, and by a Christian nation!

It matters little with which particular tribe of Anahuac the Mound-builders have become identified, since all the Nahuatl tribes were Mound-builders, and were forging a high civilization out of Nature herself.

The differentiation of the Mound-builders' intellectuality, the gradual increments of their power of specialization, would naturally improve an earth mound by facing it with stone, and in turn to build it entirely of stone, and finally truncate a solid pyramid, crown its top with a palace or a temple, and its terraces with fountains and hanging gardens. It is but natural that the pottery of the Ohio mounds, with their rude images of animals and things, would suggest the association of several such images to record a thought, and, as civilization advanced, to resolve itself into the curious hieroglyphics of the Astecs. The effigy mounds of Wisconsin were but an inherent impulse to perpetuate their symbols of worship upon the most lasting monuments known to their rude art—earth mounds. What could be more natural than that, as soon as stone temples took the place of earth mounds, they should emblazon those same symbols on the lasting rock? That same perseverance that could raise Cahokia and Grave Creek Mound has intensified itself in chiseling beautiful facades and frescoes out of solid porphyry, with no other tools than obsidian chisels. The bas-reliefs are as delicate as those cut by steel, and the paintings on the temples of Mexico of human faces, are as identical with the shape of the skulls in the museum in Chicago, with their retreating foreheads and prominent superciliary ridges, as a painting can be like a skull.

The laws of the Astecs were written in blood by a Draco, and a historian who misrepresented facts was punished with death. Accepting the above as proof evident that the paintings are correct, the large nose of the statues will forever contradict the alliance of the Astecs or Mound-builders with the Mongoloids. Hereafter we shall use the word Mound-builders as a synonym for Astecs, since we believe we have established sufficiently the analogy.

You ask, Then why have not the records of the Astecs preserved their early history in the Mississippi Valley? Such in all probability was the case, but the Spaniards burned every record they could find, and whatever history we have is fragmentary, and only such as escaped the diligence of the priests. We may marvel at first that the cupidity of the Spaniards should thus outweigh every other consideration of right and justice, but we must consider that this was the age of chivalry, just succeeding the Crusades, when all Europe turned knight-errants and went to war against the Saracens of Asia. It was the war of the Cross against the Crescent, when each Christian thought it his duty to kill a Turk, in order to plant the Cross in heathen lands.

This fever struck chivalrous Spain, and no leader could have been found more imbued with the spirit than Hernando Cortez, and it was with this spirit that he entered Mexico—to win gold for his crown and the country for his church. Iconoclasm was his creed, gold his desire, and fire and the sword his argument. When he entered the sanctuaries of their temples, and offered the sacerdotal official the image of the Virgin, in an unknown tongue, as a substitute for their tutelary divinities, on their inability to comprehend his motives, he invariably overturned their altars, broke their idols, and, with the assumption of a man ordained by Jehovah, invoked the saints to let them be anathema maranatha. No cataclysm of nature since the destruction of Atlantis has been so blighting to the growth of a nation, or so completely annihilating to their past history, as the Spanish Conquest of the New World.

Tenochtitlan, the mistress who demanded tribute of all Mexico, has vanished, and the Modern Mexico, phœnix-like, soars aloft with outstretched wings, and hovers over the earth with her music, then sinks with the last sad notes of the dying swan, to immolate herself, that she may rise from her ashes, to rise higher and sing clearer.

A Catholic cathedral occupies the place of the Teocalli, but at what cost! Ten thousand souls without the knowledge of an Evangel; the canals of the New World Venice turned into a Golgotha; the beautiful lake of Tezcuco turned into a salt marsh, the hanging gardens and fountains of princes into cactus beds, and the history of a people blotted from the face of the earth!

The modern traveler, as he looks at the changed scenes in the Valley of Mexico, may truthfully say:

*"Here didst thou fall, and here thy hunters stand
Signed in thy spoil, and crimsoned in thy lethe."*

Alfred O. Coffin

III
The Mound-builders in Central America

"Thou unrelenting Past!
Strong are the barriers round thy dark domain—
And fetters, sure and fast,
Hold all that enter thy unbreathing reign.
"Far in thy realm withdrawn,
Old empires sit in sullenness and gloom;
And glorious ages gone,
Lie deep within the shadow of thy womb.
"Full many a mighty name
Lurks in thy depth, unuttered, unrevered:
With thee are silent fame,
Forgotten arts, and wisdom disappeared."

While the Mayas of Yucatan and Central America spoke a different language from the Astecs, certain analogies in building and invention warrant us in considering them at this point. The oldest civilization in America was in Yucatan, Honduras and Guatemala, and, according to Bancroft, the oldest city in the western world is Copan, which was in ruins, deserted, and overgrown by a dense tropical forest, at the time of the Spanish Conquest, three hundred and sixty years ago.

The Mayas of Yucatan, according to their traditions, first arrived there 793 B.C. from "Tulapam." We don't know where "Tulapam" was; but they must have come by sea, because the natives of Yucatan to-day speak a language exactly similar to that spoken by the extinct aborigines of Cuba, Hayti and Jamaica, when the Spaniards first arrived there. North of Guatemala stand the ancient ruins of Palenque, the Mecca of Central America, whose facaded palaces and stuccoed temples are full of hieroglyphics and bas-reliefs, beautiful in ruins, telling the sad history of a vanished race who here offered sacrifice to Quetzalcohuatl, the nature god of the Mayas.

Nepenthe rules here supreme. A tropical forest has torn asunder her pyramids, while trees nine feet in diameter have shot up in the midst of her buildings, and nine feet of vegetable mold fill the inner courts above the pavement, where sacerdotal processions, possibly before the birth of Phœnician commerce, swung their censers and performed their mysterious rites.

A few words concerning Uxmal and its ruins will answer for the rest of Yucatan. The walls of this temple were nine feet thick, and the rich, sculptured facades are the finest in America. The sculptured portion covers twenty-four thousand square feet, while the terraced mound supporting the house contained over sixty thousand cubic yards of material; and we must remember that these people had neither metallic tools nor beasts of burden.

Nothing but the feeling of profoundest awe must fill the modern traveler, as he emerges from the depths and gloom of a tropical forest, and comes face to face with the massive walls of the pyramid of Copan, containing twenty-six million cubic feet of stone brought from a distant quarry, and whose base is six hundred and twenty-four feet by eight hundred and nine feet, with a tower one hundred and eighty-two feet, built of huge blocks of stone, surmounted by two huge trees rooted in its mold.

Within its ruins were found fourteen statues, the largest thirteen feet four inches tall, and all covered with bas-reliefs and hieroglyphics whose workmanship is equal to that on the Egyptian pyramids.

In front of the statues stand huge altars six feet square, divided into thirty-six tablets of hieroglyphics, which tell to the world their history; but they speak in an unknown tongue, so the traveler must surmise if these were the emblems of the Mayan pantheon, or the palace of a pre-Adamite man.

The curtain falls, the traveler returns, and the æons commence again their ceaseless cycles around mysterious Copan.

Alfred O. Coffin

IV
The Lost Atlantis

"Man's steps are not upon thy paths; thy fields
Are not a spoil for him; thou dost arise
And shake him from thee; the vile strength he wields
For earth's destruction thou dost all despise,
Spurning him from thy bosom to the skies,
And send him, shivering in thy playful spray,
And howling to his gods, where haply lies
His petty hope in some near port or bay,
And dash him again to earth—there let him lie."

Whence sprang the Mound-builders? It is evident, after reading the foregoing, that a people who could reach such a degree of civilization, must have received an impetus from without, which makes us conclude that the Mound-builders migrated to America.

"The Story of Atlantis," as recorded by Plato in his Timæus, has been regarded as a myth, but seems destined to become genuine history. The translation of the Greek philosopher is as follows:— "Among the great deeds of Athens, of which recollection is preserved in our books, there is one which should be placed above all others. Our books tell that the Athenians destroyed an army that came across the Atlantic Sea, and insolently invaded Europe and Asia, for this sea was then navigable, and beyond the straits where you place the Pillars of Hercules, there was an island larger than Asia (Minor) and Libya combined. From this island one could pass easily to other islands, and from these to the continent which lies around the interior sea. The sea (Mediterranean) on this side the strait of which we speak, resembles a harbor with a narrow entrance; but there is a genuine sea, and the land which surrounds it is a veritable continent. In the Island of Atlantis reigned three kings, with great and marvelous power. They had under their dominion the whole of Atlantis and other islands, and some parts of the continent. At one time their power extended into Libya, and into Europe as far as Tyrrhenia, and, uniting their whole force, they sought to destroy our whole country at a blow; but their defeat stopped the invasion and gave independence to all the countries this side the Pillars of Hercules. Afterward, in one day and one fatal night, there came mighty earthquakes and inundations which engulfed the warlike people. Atlantis disappeared beneath the sea, and then that sea became inaccessible, so that navigation on it ceased, on account of the quantity of mud which the engulfed island left in its place."

Plutarch, in his "Life of Solon," relates that the Lawgiver learned this story of Atlantis from Egyptian priests.

Diodorus Siculus relates:—"Over against Africa lies a very great island, in the vast ocean, many days' sail from Libya westward. The soil there is very fruitful, a great part whereof is mountainous, but much likewise champaign, which is the most sweet and pleasant part, for it is watered by several navigable streams, and beautiful with many gardens of pleasure, planted by divers sorts of trees and an abundance of orchards. The towns are adorned with many stately buildings and banqueting-houses, pleasantly situated in the gardens and orchards."

Theopompos, who wrote in the fourth century B.C., tells substantially the same story, which was given by Silenus to the ancient king Midas, recorded by Aristotle. The Gauls possessed traditions on this subject, which were collected by the Roman historian Timagenes, who lived in the first century before Christ. This record states that three distinct peoples dwelt in Gaul (France): (1) The indigenous population, (2) The invaders from a distant island (Atlantis), (3) The Aryan Gauls.

Marcellus, also, in a book on the Ethiopians, speaks of seven islands lying in the Atlantic Ocean near Europe, which we may undoubtedly identify with the Canaries; but he adds: "The inhabitants of these islands preserve the memory of a much greater island, Atlantis, which had, for a long time, exercised dominion over the smaller ones."

Now all these ancient writers clearly state that a continent existed west of Africa, which was destroyed by a great cataclysm. The tribes in Central America and Mexico, in Venezuela, British and Dutch Guiana, distinctly describe these cataclysms, one by water, one by fire, and a third by winds. Catlin, in his "Lifted and Subsided Rocks of America," describes the tradition of such a cataclysm.

The Abbé Brasseur de Bourbourg, in his "Quatre Lettres sur le Mexique," and "Sources de l'Histoire Primitive du Mexique," has translated the "Teo Amoxtli," which is the Toltecan mythological history of the cataclysm of the Antilles. The festival of "Izcalli" was instituted to commemorate this terrible calamity, in which "princes and people humbled themselves before the Divinity, and besought him not to renew the frightful convulsions."

It is claimed that, by this catastrophe, an area larger than France became engulfed, including the Lesser Antilles, the extensive banks at their eastern extremity, the peninsulas of Yucatan, Honduras and Guatemala, and the great estuaries of the Caribbean Sea and the Gulf of Mexico. With Yucatan and Guatemala went down the splendid cities of Palenque and Uxmal, and others whose sites and inhabitants are now in the ocean bed.

In verification of these ancient traditions, our modern geographies tell us that Old Guatemala was destroyed by a water volcano in the sixteenth century, and again in the eighteenth by an earthquake. The sea-shells on both sides of the Isthmus of Panama are alike, and according to geographical distribution of animals, this could only come about by the Isthmus having been once submerged, and after remaining so long enough for the intermixture of species, being raised; and the submarine fossils found on the Isthmus prove the hypothesis.

According to Abbé Brasseur de Bourbourg, the oldest Mexican records date back to nine hundred and twenty-five years before Christ, when a strange people came among them. In opposition to Winchell's hypothesis of a northwest Mongolian migration to Mexico, I wish to prove that the Mound-builders were the people who came after the cataclysms, and that they came from the continent of Atlantis.

And what hope have I to establish such affinity? "Dans les pays les plus différent," says Benjamin Constant, "chez les peuples de moeurs les plus opposées, le sacerdoce a dû aû culte dés éléments et des astres, un pouvoir dont audjour d'hui nous concevons à peine l'idée."

The nearest lands west of Africa, where Plato located the continent of Atlantis, are the Canary Islands, the nearest being about fifty miles from Africa, and the whole group extending about three hundred miles, and separated from the continent by a channel more than five thousand feet deep. Of all oceanic islands (not continental) discovered by Europeans, the Canaries alone were inhabited. Here were found the Guanches, now extinct, who, at the time of their discovery, were not aware that a continent existed in their neighborhood, for, on being asked by the Spanish missionaries how they had come to their archipelago, they answered: "God placed us on these islands, and then forsook and forgot us." Now who were these Guanches? Their islands have never been connected with Africa, because the channel between them is a mile deep, and Wallace, in his "Island Life," has proved that any island surrounded by water over five thousand feet deep is of volcanic origin, and that is just the clue we are seeking. If craniometry is a reliable science, the Guanches were not savages, but superior to the Egyptians! According to Prof. Flower's measurements, the skull of the English of low grade contains 1,542 cubic centimeters, the Guanches 1,498, Japanese 1,486, Chinese 1,424, Italians 1,475, and the Ancient Egyptians 1,464. That a remnant of a race found on an island in mid-ocean should have a better developed brain than many continental nations who have made history, is significant. We should expect such a people to conquer their neighbors, just as is recorded by

Plato. And now as to their dispersion. When Columbus set sail from Palos in 1492, he steered directly for the Canary Islands for repairs. When he left the Canaries, without any effort of his own the trade winds carried his vessels straight to the West Indies. These winds blow in this direction all the time. In December, 1731, a ship started from Teneriffe with a cargo of wine for one of the Western Canaries, and, having only six men on board, they were unable to manage the ship, and the trade winds carried them straight to Trinidad, on the Island of Cuba, of course. While Atlantis was sinking, some of the inhabitants escaped on rafts and boats, and, being exactly at the same point at which Columbus and the ship's crew started in the path of the trade winds, there was nothing to do but wait, and they were carried to the West Indies, through the Caribbean and Gulf of Mexico, to Yucatan and Mexico. We can easily see now why the oldest civilization of the New World is in Central America. Some of these emigrants stopped in the West Indies, for the aborigines spoke the same language as the Mayas of Yucatan to-day. Some stopped in South America, for Dr. Lund, the eminent Swedish naturalist, in the bone caves of Minas Gerais, Brazil, found human skulls exactly like those of the Mound-builders.

The sudden destruction of these people recalls the beautiful lines from Richardson's Geology, on "The Nautilus and the Ammorite:"

"They sailed all day, through creek and bay,
And traversed the ocean deep;
And at night they sank on a coral bed,

In its fairy bowers to sleep.
"And the monsters vast, of ages past,
They beheld in their ocean caves;
They saw them ride, in their power and pride,
And sink in their deep sea graves.

"And they came at last, to a sea long past;
But as they reached its shore,
The Almighty's breath spoke out in death,
And the Ammorite breathed no more."

V
Deductions

We now proceed to discuss the relation of the Mound-builders to the inhabitants of Atlantis, or their immediate neighbors, the Egyptians. Dr. Waitz, in his "Anthropology of Primitive Peoples," observes: "The first elements of civilization, as far as history reaches, always appear as communicated from one people to another; and of no people can it be proved how, where and when they have become civilized by their own inherent power." Now, Winchell in his genealogical charts, represents the entire peopling of the Pacific Slope from Alaska to Chili by Mongoloid branches, and the world knows that the civilization of the Chinese is and has always been a petrified fossil. The race is absolutely devoid of civilizing qualities. Their state is founded upon the worship of the shades of their ancestors. Their exalted egotism has for ages resisted every attempt to force advancement among them, and the only thing that we can call development among them is atavism.

To say that such a people gave rise to the Esquimaux, is to verify all history; to say that they are the source of the Astec civilization and Inca sun-worship, is to perpetuate an anthropological paradox.

Empiricism alone holds but a secondary place in establishing scientific truth, and all à priori reasoning must hold precedence, when analogy and affinity would supplement the existing links of discontinued evidence.

Separated by a channel only fifty miles wide, we may with justice assume that the civilization of Atlantis and Egypt was very similar. Egypt is the only land of the ancient world where pyramids are found. On a direct line of the trade winds, in Yucatan, Guatemala, Honduras, Mexico and the Ohio Valley, we find other pyramids. In Egypt we find the temple emblazoned with hieroglyphics chiseled in the solid rock, describing the history of one of the oldest civilizations in the world. In Uxmal, Mexico, Copan and Palenque are tablets, friezes, bas-reliefs, facades and hieroglyphics; though inferior to the Egyptians' in mimetic art, still of the highest order, considering this to be the product of the Neolithic Age.

The Egyptians were the only people of the Old World who embalmed their dead. According to the French historian, Lucien Bart, the Zapotecs and Chichimecs of the Mexican Valley embalmed their chiefs, and if we may believe this author, the caves of the Cordilleras are vast museums, as full of interest as the catacombs of Rome.

That the Americans mummified their dead, is proven by mummies having been found in Peru and the northwestern part of Patagonia. Dr. Aq. Reid has found others which prove the relation of Peruvian civilization to that of Patagonia.

One of these mummies has been deposited in the museum of Ratisbon, Bavaria, and another was sent to the Smithsonian Institute. (vid. Aq. Reid, Smithsonian Annual Report, 1862, pp. 87, 426.) This mummy led to the remark of Alexander Winchell: "The humid atmosphere of Patagonia leads to the inference that the mummification of the dead was practiced under the influence of some controlling motive, which must have been inherited from ancestors dwelling in a more propitious clime, and from which even the dripping meteorology of Patagonia was insufficient to eradicate." The Egyptians were accurate astrologers and astronomers. They accurately calculated eclipses and the reappearances of stars whose reappearance would require over a thousand years, and the pyramids are set to the cardinal points. Less than a hundred years ago, the great Calendar Stone of the Astecs was dug up, in the City of Mexico. It is of a solid piece of porphyry, and weighs fifty tons. It was brought many leagues, across a broken country, without beasts of burden, and Bustamente states that ten thousand men were employed in its transportation. The Calendar Stone was buried when Cortez sacked the city of Tenochtitlan, and in itself constitutes a history. From it we learn that the Astecs were astrologers, astronomers, and calculated eclipses, and knew the solstices of the sun. They divided the year into eighteen months of twenty days each, and like the ancient Egyptians, had five complementary days to make out the three hundred and sixty-five, and every fifty-two years they threw in twelve and one-half days for leap year. Like the Persians and Egyptians, a cycle of fifty-two years, or "an age," was represented by a serpent, so prominent in ancient mythology. Their astrological year was divided into months of thirteen days each, and there were thirteen years in their indications, which contained each three hundred and sixty-five periods of thirteen days. It is also curious, that their number of lunar months of thirteen days, contained in a cycle of fifty-two years, with the intercalation of thirteen (twelve and one-half) days, should correspond exactly with the number of years in a great Sothic period of the Egyptians, viz:—fourteen hundred and ninety-one.

Is it reasonable to suppose that this strange affinity with Egyptian civilization was accidental? or that a Turanian branch independently evolved itself into a counterpart of Hamitic Berbers? Hardly.

The ideographic paintings of the Astecs or Mound-builders preserve traditions of the creation of the world, a universal flood, confusion of tongues and dispersion of men, and that a single man and woman saved themselves in a boat which landed near Mount Colhuacan, and that all their children were born deaf, and remained so till a dove one day, from the top of a tree, taught them each in a different tongue. All Astec traditions, without exception, insist that they came from a far-off island called Aztlan (Atlantis). Dr. Lapham, in his "Antiquities of Wisconsin," locates "Azatland" in Wisconsin, on account of the large number of effigy mounds found there, and Dr. Foster, in his "Prehistoric Races," figures these mounds called "Azatland," but the Astec painting published by Gemellé Carera, in his Giro del Mondo, has hieroglyphics representing their departure from Aztlan in canoes and on rafts, after the confusion of tongues, and a teocalli, or temple, by the side of a palm-tree. Now we all know palms do not grow in Wisconsin, but they do grow in Africa.

Max Müller, the world's greatest authority in philology, says, that of all indices to the mysteries of the ancient world, language is the most satisfactory, and the only evidence worth listening to with regard to ante-historic periods.

If we class the languages of the world into groups according to cognation, we find the Aryan languages comprising the Indian, Persian (Sanskrit), Hellenic, Latin group (Italian, Wallachian, Provencal, French, Portuguese and Spanish), Slavonic (Russian), Teutonic (English), and the Keltic or Welsh, of which the oldest is the Sanskrit and Zend.

The Semitic group comprises the Hebrew, Phœnician, Assyrian and Arabic, while the Babylonian and Chinese stand alone. The Aryan and Semitic form a class known as the inflectional, and are the only languages of the world that are adapted to and possess a literature, and that have advanced the progress of the world in religion, arts, or sciences.

Though springing from a common center, they have grammatical structures that prevent the one being derived from the other. The Semitic branched southward and westward, and was the language of the Chaldee, Arab, Hebrew and Egyptian, the latter sometimes classed as Hamitic. The Chinese is an inorganic language, monosyllabic, and destitute of all grammar. The nouns have no number, declensions or cases, and the verbs are without conjugation through moods, tenses and persons. All Mongoloid races that reached North America must have done so by Behring's Strait, and all such races or descendants would undoubtedly have a trace of their parental language. If the Mound-builders or Astecs were derived from Mongoloids, we should expect a monosyllabic language, but, on the contrary, "The Astec language has more diminutives and augmentatives than the Italian, and its substantives and verbs are more numerous than in any other language." Another proof of its wealth is, that when missionaries first went among them, they found no trouble in expressing abstract ideas like religion, virtue, etc.

The Sanskrit word God is Devan; the Latin, Deus; the Greek, Θεός, and the Astec word is Teotl. Whether this similarity in sound and spelling was accidental or constitutional, I know not, but comparative philology recognizes radical rather than phonetic affinities.

The Pythagorean doctrine of transmigration of souls was the ruling passion among the Astecs. Whether this was the fruition of all polytheistic religions, or the retention of primordial culture, I know not; but we know the Egyptians embalmed their dead, lest the dissolution of the body would destroy also the soul, and the greatest desecration that could befall the ancient Greeks and Romans was the refusal of burial, because the soul of him thus uncared for wandered thenceforth as a disembodied ghost. We read in Homer's "Iliad" how the dead Patroclus comes to the sleeping Achilles, who tries in vain to grasp him with loving arms, but the soul, like smoke, flits away below the earth. How Hermotimos, the seer, used to go out of his body, till at last, his soul, coming back from a spirit journey, found that his wife had burnt his body on a funeral pile, and that he had become a bodyless ghost. How Odysseus visits the bloodless ghosts in Hades, and the shadows of the dead in Purgatory wondered to see the body of Dante there, which stopped the sunlight and cast a shadow.

This idea of the phantom life of souls as shades and shadows constitutes the higher philosophy of the transcendental metaphysics of the ancient Greeks, whose exponent was Pythagoras.

Forbearing to enter here upon the religious status of the Astecs, we turn again to their language. If we are to believe the highest authority on these subjects, we are ready to prove that the Atlas Mountains and Atlantic Ocean, while known to the Greeks a thousand years before Christ, still belong to the Nahuatl language in North America.

The words Atlas and Atlantic have no satisfactory etymology in any language in Europe or Asia, and we are certain no such roots are found in the Greek; but in the Nahuatl language we find their homes.

The consonants most used are l, t, x, z; next the sounds tl and tz; but l, the most frequent used, is never found at the beginning of a word.

The radicals a, atl, which signify water, atlan, on the border or amid the water, give us the adjective Atlantic, pertaining to the land, Aztlan (or Atlantis), in the midst of the water. We have also atlaca, to hurl or dart from the water, whose preterite makes atlaz. In the time of Columbus a city named Atlan existed on the Gulf of Darien, with a good harbor, but now it is only a small pueblo named Acla.

Undoubtedly we have reached the fountain-head. The nearest point of land from the Island of "Atlantis" was the Atlas Mountains, which at that distance would seem to be darted up from the water; from their Atlantis, in the midst of the water. One has but to look on the map of Mexico to-day, and see that my theory is supported by such words as Tlascoran, Tlascala, Tlatlanquitepec, Tlascopan, Tenochtitlan, Chialinitzla, Yxtacamaxtitlan, Popocatapetl, etc., and scores of others, which prove that those combinations of liquids and consonants are at home only in the Nahuatl countries; ergo, the Atlas Mountains and Atlantic Ocean and "Atlantis" were named by these people before their continent was destroyed.

VI
The First Men of America

"Antiquity appears to have begun long after their primeval race was run."

Time is the only alembic to test the true character of great men or deeds. Homer, Dante, Shakespeare, Goethe and Hugo are the few select representatives whom the world acknowledges as its spokesmen. Shakespeare was in his grave a hundred years before he spoke authoritatively to the world, and with Dante it was no better. Ages had passed away before the seven cities of Greece warred for the honor of Homer's birthplace, but for twenty-six centuries has the "Siege of Troy" stood out in profile as the model epic of the world, but of doubtful veracity because of its antiquity; but Dr. Schliemann's excavations seem destined yet to find the funeral pyre of Patroclus, surrounded by the remains of Trojan captives.

Even within the last twelve months has the French archæologist, M. Marcel Dieulafay, brought to light the ancient city of Susa, and we may now behold the palace of Artaxerxes Mnemon, whose foundation was laid by Xerxes I. 485 B.C.; and now, after twenty-three centuries, the Bible student may take his Bible in his hand and turn to the Book of Esther and read, while the guide in the ancient capital of Persia points to this spot where Mordecai sat, to that spot where Haman was hanged, to this Court where the lovely Esther was crowned queen, and whence the sorrowing Vashti departed, as the unfortunate Hebe, cupbearer of Jove, before the victorious Ganymede.

Plato recorded the sad fate of Atlantis nearly five hundred years before Christ, and Solon had recorded the same in a poem two hundred years before. Plato says the expedition against Egypt took place during the reigns of the Athenian kings, Cecrops and Erechtheus, and according to the "Marble of Paros," those kings ruled in 1582 B.C. and 1409 B.C., which is not a great deal more ancient than the siege of Troy.

Though this is ancient history, we have as much right to accept Plato's history as Homer's, if it can be established.

The Abbé Brasseur de Bourbourg claims that Mexican chronology dates back two thousand eight hundred and fourteen years. Because America was latest discovered, it is the popular opinion that it should have been the latest developed, but there is evidence sufficient that the New World is in every sense the oldest.

We know that this continent was once covered with glaciers as low down as New Jersey and the Ohio River. According to Dr. Croll, glaciation is brought about by the combined effect of the eccentricity of the earth's orbit and the precession of the equinoxes, which makes the distance of our planet from the sun vary considerably during the year. We are three million miles nearer the sun in winter than in summer, while the reverse is the case in the Southern Hemisphere. If our winter now were long as our summer, and we were to continue three million miles nearer the sun in the winter, a decided change would occur, and our winters would grow longer and colder, and our summers shorter and hotter. Now the precession of the equinoxes and the motion of aphelion actually bring this about every ten thousand five hundred years, and the condition of the two hemispheres is reversed as regards their glaciation, and this reversion has been going on during all geologic time.

But the eccentricity itself of the earth in its orbit between perihelion and aphelion varies, and since the eccentricity is now at its minimum, three million miles, we infer that our last glacial epoch occurred ten thousand five hundred years ago, and the ice mantle has retreated from 39° in New Jersey to 61° in Southern Greenland, which is now covered by a glacier twelve hundred miles long, four hundred miles wide, and a mile thick, while the ice in the Southern Hemisphere has increased to several miles in thickness, and to such extent, that the nearest point to the South Pole Sir Ross was able to reach, was still fourteen hundred miles from the Pole.

While the St. Lawrence and the area of the Great Lakes were under these glaciers, of course there could have been no outlet to the Atlantic of the waters, which were forced by the Alleghenies to flow to the Gulf, at the time of the great thaw ten thousand years ago, and the St. Lawrence could only have been formed after the ice had retreated beyond the Great Lake areas. Since that period the Niagara has been cutting its way from Lake Ontario through the solid limestone of the Upper Silurian Period, until the Falls of Niagara are now seven miles from the lake. Dana estimates that the river has cut its way at the rate of a foot a year, which would make it thirty-five thousand years cutting its channel. Sir Charles Lyell, as quoted in Hugh Miller's "Testimony of the Rocks," estimates the rate at fifty yards in forty years, which would make it ten thousand years, which agrees exactly with the time the glacier crossed the Great Lakes. However long it was, man was here then, for a tooth of a man has been found with that of a mammoth in the Drift of the Niagara, and Dr. Abbott has found bones of the mastodon and the wisdom tooth of a man, fourteen feet under the gravel of the Delaware, and their rolled and abraded surfaces prove them either pre-glacial or contemporaneous with glaciers.

While the great glaciers were breaking up at the head-waters of the Platte, Yellowstone and Missouri, the flooded rivers dropped their sediment in the vast inundated lakes, whose rich bottoms formed the loess which so well characterizes the fertile prairie soil of the Western States to-day.

In Nebraska, stone arrow-heads and the bones of the ancient elephant were found thirty feet under the loess, and in Greene County, Illinois, a well was dug seventy-two feet through the loess, when a stone hatchet was found, proving that the hatchet was dropped there when Illinois was covered by a lake over which the rude hunter paddled his canoe.

Dr. Koch, of St. Louis, found the bones of the mastodon in the Osage Valley in Missouri, which was killed while mired down, by fire being built around it, which consumed nearly all the bones of the animal except the legs and toes. The presence of ashes and stones proves conclusively that the huge animal met his death at the hands of man.

One other instance to prove that man existed on this continent in the Pliocene Epoch: Dr. Winslow sent to the Natural History

Society, of Boston, a skull of a human being found in a shaft in California one hundred and eighty feet deep, and under five successive layers of volcanic lava and tufa and four layers of auriferous gravel. To quote from Foster's "Prehistoric Times": "Since the introduction, then, of man on this continent, the physical features as well as the climate have undergone great changes. The volcanic peaks of the Sierra Nevadas have been lifted up, the glaciers have disappeared, the great cañons themselves have been excavated in the solid rock, and what then were the beds of streams, now form the Table Mountains." Admitting this skull to be Pliocene, we have a human bone in America older than the oldest human relics found on the continent of Europe. When we consider that this skull was in situ before the mainland of the Sierras was uplifted by volcanic upheavals, accompanied by flaming rivers of molten lava, followed by the glacial night of cold, ice and snow, we no longer believe that the first inhabitants of North America crossed Behring's Strait from Asia.

We have argued that the Mound-builders both entered and left the Mississippi Valley by the south, and that the Red Indian entered by Florida from the Antilles, as implements found in Jamaica correspond with those found in Venezuela, and DeSoto found a higher civilization among the Natchez tribes of the South than was found among any others.

According to the Icelandic sagas, Lief and Bjorn reached Labrador about the year 1000 A.D. and found a dwarfish race of men "of short stature," whom they called skraelings. We know well such terms could not apply to the stately Algonquin warriors the

Europeans found in New England. No; these were Esquimaux, whom the warlike Indians had compelled to follow the retreat of the glaciers toward the Land of the Midnight Sun. They crossed to the Great Lakes and compelled the peaceful Mound-builders to go southward. They crossed the Rocky Mountains and drove the inhabitants of the Sierras also. They crowded them into the gorges and cañons of Colorado, Utah and Arizona. The frightened refugees were driven to the necessity of building dwellings in the overhanging cliffs of rivers, and these nests of human swallows are now known as the "Cliff-dwellers" of the Colorado and Hili.

They were not allowed to stay here. Driven by their relentless hunters, they moved onward to the plateaus of Arizona and cactus plains of New Mexico, where, huddled up between the tribes of Mexico on the south, and the hunting Indians behind them, they built the pueblos and "The Seven Cities of Cibola." The archæological remains prove to us to-day that New Mexico was as thickly settled by these miserable fugitives as Pennsylvania or Delaware. The mournful spectacle to-day of the adobe pueblos along the Pecos and Rio Grande, is the closing chapter of a history written in blood, and sealed by the life of a nation, with characters forever enigmatical to the civilized world.

VII
Conclusion

"And thy request think now fulfilled, that asked how first this world and face of things began, and what before thy memory was done from the beginning."

The former existence of Atlantis is an hypothesis, it is true, but so is the existence of Lemuria, and nearly every scientist of Europe believes that a continent once existed in the Indian Ocean between Madagascar and India, and the proof is not wanting.

On the Island of Madagascar are found thirty-three species of monkeys, called Lemurs, which are not found in Africa, nor in any other part of the globe, except Ceylon, India, and the Malay Archipelago. Because the Lemurs are found only in this region, Sclater, the English zoölogist, has called the sunken continent "Lemuria."

Between Madagascar and India are a number of submerged banks of less than one thousand fathoms deep, which a slight elevation would make comparative easy stages of communication between Madagascar and India for all animals. An elevation of three hundred feet would unite Java, Sumatra and Borneo into one great peninsula of the Asiatic continent.

The Island of Madagascar is two hundred and fifty miles wide and one thousand miles long, and is separated from Africa by the Mozambique Channel, only two hundred and fifty miles wide. Africa has monkeys, apes, and baboons; also lions, leopards, hyenas, zebras, rhinocerii, elephants, buffaloes, giraffes, and many species of deer and antelopes; but strange to say, not one of these animals is found in Madagascar, or anything like them. There are in Madagascar, according to Wallace's "Island Life," and Dr. Hartlaub's "Birds of Madagascar," one hundred species of land birds, and only four or five have any kindred in Africa; but in Malaysia and India we find identical species, and on the islands of Mauritius, Rodriguez, Bourbon and the Seychelles group we find so many curious birds without wings, with similar kindred in Madagascar, that we know these islands have been connected.

The Seychelles group, two hundred by three hundred miles in extent, are seven hundred miles northeast from Madagascar, and have fifteen peculiar species of birds, while three of them are found in Madagascar, and some have kindred in India.

There are five species of lizards which are found in Mauritius, Bourbon, Rodriguez and Ceylon, and even to the Philippine Islands.

The Mascarene group contains one thousand and fifty-eight species of plants, of which sixty-six are found in Africa but not in Asia, and eighty-six are found in Asia and not in Africa, showing a closer relation to Asia than to Africa. Milne-Edwards has even surmised a "Mascarene" continent, to include all the outlying islands around Madagascar. Beccari, in his work on the geographical distribution of palms, after noting the difficulties of the dispersion of the fruits, reaches the conclusion that, when we find two congeneric species of palms on widely separated lands, it is reasonable to infer that these lands have been united. On the Mascarene Islands, in Ceylon, the Nicobars, at Singapore, on the

Malaccas, New Guinea, in Australia and Polynesia occur various species of Phychosperma, all very difficult of dissemination, and hence could have reached their present habitat only by being connected by intervening lands now in the ocean bed. Winchell, in his "Pre-Adamites," states among his principles: 1st, The doctrine of pre-Adamites is entirely consonant with the fundamental principles of Biblical Christianity; 2d, A chain of profound relationship runs through the constitution of all races, and they may be regarded as genealogically connected together; 3d, The initial point of the genealogical line may be located in Lemuria.

Peschell, in his "Races of Man," says: "This continent, which would correspond with the Indian Ethiopia of Claudius Ptolemæus, is required by anthropology, for we can then conceive how the inferior populations of Australia and India, the Papuans of the East India Islands, and lastly the Negroes, would thus be enabled to reach their present abode by dry land." The selection of this spot is far more orthodox than it might at the first glance appear, for we here find ourselves in the neighborhood of the four enigmatical rivers of the scriptural Eden—in the vicinity of the Nile, Euphrates, Tigris and Indus. By the gradual submergence of Lemuria, the expulsion from Paradise would also be inexorably accomplished. To this he adds the arguments of such ecclesiastical writers as Lactantius, the venerable Bede, Hrabanus Maurus, Cosmas Indicopleustes and the anonymous geographer of Ravenna. In the second chapter of Genesis we read: "A river went out of Eden to water the garden, and from thence it was parted and came into four heads." Whether such a river exists to-day, I know not. Dr. McCausland, in his "Adam and

Adamite," believes that Eden was on the west bank of the modern Euphrates, near the Persian Gulf. He says the Pison river of Genesis, in conjunction with the modern Karùn, is the Pasitigris of the ancients, which runs through the country of Evilat or Havillah, and flows into the Euphrates before it falls into the Persian Gulf. The second is the modern Karashú, the Gyndes of the ancients, which traverses the land of Cush. The Hiddekel is plainly the Tigris, and is designated in Daniel x. 4, and runs westward to Assyria.

We know by the remains of sea-shells that the Great Desert of Sahara was once the bottom of the ocean, and its elevation may have been consonant with and the direct cause of the submergence of Lemuria.

Alfred Wallace says none but the unscientific have revived Atlantis since Darwin's "Origin of Species" and Prof. Asa Grey on "The Affinity of North American and Asiatic Floras." It is not my desire to pose as unscientific, nor to construct a highway for the Polearctic or Nearctic fauna and flora, but to prove that the anthropological and ethnological affinities of the Nahuatl tribes deserve a newer and better classification; and if the restoration of Atlantis will accomplish that end, then let the theory stand or fall on its merits.

If Lemuria can be established by affinity, why not accept as much of such collateral evidence concerning Atlantis as is compatible with science.

The Pacific Ocean is not stormy. Winchell says South America was peopled by Mongoloids from the Polynesian Islands. Since no storms prevail there, the theory would indicate a design on the inhabitants to seek new shores, which lay so many hundred miles away, across a sea where storms would never carry them by accident; but in the peopling of Central America from the East, the stormy Atlantic and unvarying trade winds would carry any unwary voyager who strayed too far from shore. As to the establishing of scientific data in support of Atlantis, I have to add that it is probably a short while before the acceptance will be as universal as Lemuria.

In 1873 Her Majesty's ship Challenger made soundings in the Atlantic off the north coast of Africa, and in 1874 the German frigate Gazelle made further soundings in the same region.

In 1877 Commander Gorringe, of the U. S. sloop Gettysburg, discovered, about one hundred and fifty miles from the Straits of Gibraltar, an immense bed of pink coral in thirty-two fathoms of water.

"These various series of soundings, when located on a map, indicate the existence of an extended bank of comparatively shallow water, in the midst of which the Canaries and the Madeiras rise to the surface. The location of the newly discovered mountain in the Atlantic lies within the fifteen-thousand-fathom line, and here is probably the stump of the ancient Atlantis."

www.ingramcontent.com/pod-product-compliance
Lightning Source LLC
Chambersburg PA
CBHW072210100526
44589CB00015B/2455